Amazing Nature

Ferocious Fighters

Tim Knight

Heinemann
LIBRARY

www.heinemann.co.uk/library
Visit our website to find out more information about **Heinemann Library** books.

To order:
☎ Phone 44 (0) 1865 888066
▤ Send a fax to 44 (0) 1865 314091
▢ Visit the Heinemann Bookshop at www.heinemann.co.uk/library to browse our catalogue and order online.

First published in Great Britain by Heinemann Library, Halley Court, Jordan Hill, Oxford OX2 8EJ, part of Harcourt Education.
Heinemann is a registered trademark of Harcourt Education Ltd.

Editorial: Jilly Attwood and Claire Throp
Design: David Poole and Geoff Ward
Picture Research: Peter Morris
Production: Séverine Ribierre

Originated by Ambassador Litho Ltd
Printed and bound in Hong Kong, China by South China Printing Company

ISBN 0 431 16651 X
07 06 05 04 03
10 9 8 7 6 5 4 3 2 1

British Library Cataloguing in Publication Data
Knight, Tim
Ferocious Fighters - (Amazing Nature)
591.5'66
A full catalogue record for this book is available from the British Library.

Acknowledgements
The Publishers would like to thank the following for permission to reproduce photographs:
Bruce Coleman pp. 13 (Jorg & Petra Wegner), **15t** (Rod Williams), **17b** (Rita Meyer), **20** (Jeff Foott), **21**, **27** (Jane Burton); Corbis pp. **10** (Kevin Schafer), **24** (Kennan Ward); FLPA pp. **5** (Philip Perry), **6** (David Hosking), **7** (W Wisniewski), **8** (T & P Gardner), **25** (Albert Visage); NHPA pp. **4-5**, **9**, **18** (Martin Harvey), **12** (Andy Rouse), **15b** (Gerard Lacz), **17t** (G I Bernard), **22** (Jonathan and Angela Scott), **23** (T Kitchin & V Hurst), **26** (Daniel Heuclin); Tim Knight pp. **11**, **14**, **16**, **19**

Cover photograph of two kangaroos, reproduced with permission of NHPA.

Every effort has been made to contact copyright holders of any material reproduced in this book. Any omissions will be rectified in subsequent printings if notice is given to the Publishers.

Contents

Any words appearing in the text in bold, **like this**, are explained in the Glossary.

Fighting for survival

Animals fight because they have to. From the largest elephant to the tiniest insect, every creature must fight to survive. Hungry and thirsty animals fight over food and water. Their lives depend on these things, so it is worth fighting hard for them. If food and water are in short supply, animals may have to fight their own kind. When they are looking for a new place to live, animals have to fight each other if they want the best **territory**. When they are ready to **mate**, males often fight over females.

Animals do not just fight their own kind. Other enemies may attack or threaten them. Many animals will fight to protect themselves or their family.

Prizefighters

Life in the animal kingdom is like a competition. The animals have to fight for prizes, such as food or the best territory. Only the strongest will win these prizes. The fighting never ends. It is very hard to catch food, find a home and attract a mate, so most animals will fight time after time just to keep what they have.

Two gemsbok males use their horns to fight.

A thirsty elephant will drive away other animals to avoid sharing a precious waterhole.

Why fight?

Animals may have to fight for many reasons. Some fights are nothing more than family squabbles. Others are all-out war between bitter enemies.

Family feuds

Many animals live in **extended families**, with aunts, uncles, cousins and grandparents. With so many close relatives crowded together, fights are bound to break out. Most are small squabbles but some fights are more serious. If food is very scarce, lions in the same **pride** may fight over a kill. Normally, the rest of the pride waits until the biggest lions have eaten their fill. This kind of food queue is known as a **pecking order**.

Any animal that tries to drive a fully-grown lion from its meal is in danger of being killed itself.

Civil war

Neighbouring families may fight each other. The fights are usually about **territory**. Sometimes a small group from a monkey **troop** will organize raiding parties to steal females from their **rivals'** camp. In most fights over territory, the bigger family will win. In a **colony** of weaverbirds, fights often break out over the best nest sites. The losers have to build their nests within reach of snakes and other **predators** that may eat the birds' eggs and young.

Alien invaders

Some animals may live peacefully side by side, but they do not let strangers come near. Nesting colonies of skuas, terns and other seabirds dive-bomb humans who get too close. Songbirds join together to drive away a dangerous bird of prey by **mobbing** it.

Some animals and birds, like this Pomarine skua, have to protect their nests against human intruders.

Avoiding a fight

Fighting uses a lot of time and energy. Animals need this energy for other activities. Fighting is also dangerous because the animals may be injured. Most animals prefer to concentrate on eating, **mating** and raising a family, and they will only fight as a last resort. The best way to avoid trouble is to stay away from your **rivals** and enemies in the first place.

Blind mole-rats live in tunnels underground. Outside the **breeding season**, blind mole-rats prefer to be alone. If two mole-rats meet by accident, they may fight to the death. They avoid each other by banging their heads on the tunnel roof and listening for a reply. Blind mole-rats have no ears, so they have to lean against the tunnel wall and feel the vibrations.

Tigers live and hunt alone. They usually fight if they meet, so they avoid close encounters by leaving claw and scent marks around their territory.

It's a gas

Some animals mark their **territory** with strong scent. This helps them to avoid bumping into each other by mistake. When bushbabies are ready to leave their daytime shelter, they spray urine on their hands and feet. As the bushbabies climb through the branches in search of food, they cover their private patch of forest with a trail of stinky paw prints.

Groups of ring-tailed lemurs patrol the edge of their home range. They mark some of the trees with scent. These scenting posts act like temporary 'keep out' signs, which warn rivals not to cross the smelly border. Sometimes rival groups of lemurs do see each other. If so, each group stands on either side of an invisible line. They rub scent into their long tails and wave them at their enemy, trying to gas each other out.

A ring-tailed lemur prepares for a 'stink fight' with its neighbours.

War of words

Some animals prefer to stay far away from their **rivals**. They defend their **territory** or warn their rivals to stay away by having long-range shouting matches or even singing competitions.

Every forest has its very own tree-top choir. The rainforests of south-east Asia are filled with the sound of rival gibbon **troops**. Their whooping calls tell each other to 'keep out'. South American howler monkeys have the loudest call of any land animal. Every morning and evening, they sing in chorus together. Making a racket like this warns other howler troops not to invade their territory.

A young howler monkey joins in with the cries of the adults in its troop.

Each kind of cicada has a different call, so the forest is filled with a variety of buzzing, whining and trumpeting noises.

Insects also fight their battles using sound rather than physical violence. Male cicadas challenge each other using their ear-splitting call. The call of the cicada is one of the most deafening sounds in the insect world. Cicadas produce the sound in a part of the body called a tymbal. The tymbal vibrates hundreds of times a second and produces an incredible noise.

The sound of drums

Sometimes it is easier to make sounds using a tool. Elephants that live in thick forest, rather than the open **savannah**, communicate by using tree trunks as drums. When a pair of Australian palm cockatoos take over a new territory, one of the birds bangs a drum to announce their arrival. The bird breaks off a stick and beats it against a hollow tree.

Practice makes perfect

Most animals prefer to avoid trouble, but they need to be ready for the day when they have no choice but to fight. While baby animals are growing up, they often rely on their parents to defend them. As they grow older, they will have to learn to fight their own battles. Animals do not become great fighters overnight. To build up their strength they begin play fighting at an early age. They practise their fighting skills with members of their own family.

When bear cubs play-fight, they avoid using their sharp claws, just like a friendly cat playing with its owner.

Learning

When both playmates refuse to back down, a fight may turn serious. The loser still learns a valuable lesson. For example, if a chimpanzee is beaten up every time he bites an older brother, he soon learns not to pick on anyone bigger or stronger. Play fighting helps young animals to work out their place in the **pecking order**. It also teaches them not to fight battles that they cannot win.

*A baby gorilla sometimes stands on its hind legs and beats its chest. These actions are just like those made by the **dominant** male gorilla in his group.*

Warning signs

Sooner or later, most enemies or **rivals** will meet face to face. This does not mean that the two sides will fight. They may just want to take a closer look at each other and weigh up their chances of success. More often than not, they simply show off their weapons or try to scare each other. This behaviour is known as **threat display**.

Some warning signs are obvious. A silverback gorilla roars, beats his chest, and shakes the bushes around him. Chameleons puff up their bodies and even turn black with anger. Other warning signals are easy to miss, unless you watch carefully. Raised eyebrows may be the only warning a macaque monkey gives before flinging itself at an enemy.

When a hippopotamus yawns, it is preparing to attack, not fall asleep.

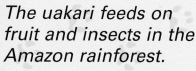
The uakari feeds on fruit and insects in the Amazon rainforest.

monkey Links

Mandrills and uakaris are distant cousins from different countries, but their painted faces send the same warning message.

Mandrills are found in West Africa. They roam the forest floor in large troops led by a **dominant** male.

War paint

For larger animals, such as monkeys, bright colours are like war paint. They can help a powerful male to scare his rivals by showing them that he is ready for battle. To us, the red-faced uakari from South America may look strange. To other uakaris, the bright scarlet head says 'Don't mess with me!'

Animals often make sure their weapons can be clearly seen. A male baboon displays his sharp teeth with a big yawn. It is good to show your **opponent** exactly how strong you are, so that he admits defeat before the real fighting has even started.

15

Tests of strength

Once **rivals** have had a good look at each other, it is usually obvious that one of them is stronger. The weaker animal may give up. The clear favourite wins without a fight. The real trouble starts when both sides think that they can win. It is still possible for animals to avoid a serious injury, even at this late stage. They do this by taking part in **ritual combat**, which tests their strength without causing too much damage.

Ritual combat

Giraffes have their own type of ritual combat. Instead of trying to hurt each other with sharp kicks from their hooves, giraffes fight by **necking**. They stand side by side, swing their necks back and then slam them into each other. Whoever knocks their **opponent** off balance wins the contest. In the early stages of a fight, the animals test each other out. They search for a weakness that would help them win. It may not look like much of a fight, but every move is vital. The **tactics** become more and more aggressive at each stage of the fight. Either fighter can back down at any time if he feels that he is about to lose.

Necking fights help young male giraffes to work out which animal is stronger.

Strawberry poison frogs push and shove each other in a fight over territory.

Many kinds of animal take part in ritual contests. Dazzlingly coloured poison-dart frogs hold wrestling matches. They slip and slide on the wet **leaf litter** as they try to push each other over. Male zebras avoid making an all-out attack on their rival until they have tested each other first. They bite each other's legs and ears and neck-wrestle to see which one is the stronger.

Zebra fights sometimes go no further than a bit of ear-nibbling.

Unarmed combat

When animals fight, they do not always use their strongest weapons. The more dangerous their weapons are, the more important it is for **rivals** to fight carefully.

Rival kangaroos first try to settle a fight by using their front paws as boxing gloves. One kick from their powerful hind legs could rip open their **opponent's** stomach, so they avoid kicking, unless neither side admits defeat.

When male red kangaroos are fighting for the right to mate with a female, they usually settle their argument with a boxing match.

No biting, no stinging

The fangs of a striking rattlesnake carry enough **venom** to kill a horse, but male rattlesnakes never bite each other when they fight over a female. Instead, they perform a kind of dance. They rear up side by side and try to pin each other to the ground. The losing snake simply crawls away. Why? Experience has taught the rattlesnake that fighting with deadly weapons is risky. Once you try to bite your opponent, there is always a chance that he might defend himself by biting you first.

The rules of the game vary depending on the type of animal, but the principle is always the same. Whether you're a wrestling frog, a boxing kangaroo, or a dancing snake, it is best to avoid real violence, such as biting, scratching, stinging or kicking, unless it is absolutely necessary.

Rival scorpions fight by locking their front claws together and pushing each other around. If they simply tried to sting each other to death, they might both be killed.

Dangerous weapons

Different animals use different parts of their bodies for fighting. Those with sharp teeth and claws will bite and scratch. Others stab or head-butt each other instead.

Bull walruses fight other males with their tusks (a pair of long, pointed teeth more than a metre long). Their thick, wrinkly skin protects them from serious injury. This kind of fighting is known as **jousting**.

Battering rams

Sometimes, an animal's own head makes a useful weapon. Bighorn rams in the deserts of the USA settle an argument by charging straight at each other. They can reach a combined speed of 65 kilometres per hour. Their violent head-on collisions sound like a thunderclap. These head-bangers only survive because they have very thick skull bones, which cushion the blow like built-in crash helmets.

Bighorn rams go head to head to decide who is boss.

During the mating season, known as the rut, stags grow antlers. The older and more powerful the stag, the bigger his weapons. Large antlers warn other males to keep their distance, and show the females that he is worth knowing.

The bull moose, the giant of the deer family, has the biggest antlers of all. They grow up to 2 metres across and are tipped with vicious spikes that can **inflict** serious stab wounds.

Rhinoceros beetles and stag beetles have horns too, but fighting males do not stab each other. Instead, they grab their opponent, lift him off the ground, and throw him to one side.

You win

Once the real fighting begins, it is usually obvious which of the two animals is stronger. Some fights are so one-sided that they are over in seconds. For example, a young male in a **troop** of monkeys may push his luck too far and take a severe beating from the group leader.

A single hyena may make a half-hearted attempt to steal a leopard's kill, but it will slink away with a yelp. If it returns with more hyenas, things are different. Once a crowd of **scavenging** hyenas gathers, the leopard has no choice but to back off. A weak or outnumbered animal needs to stop fighting as soon as possible, in order to avoid serious injury.

An angry cape buffalo weighing up to 800 kilograms is too much for one lion to handle.

A defeated wolf rolls over and begs for mercy.

Surrender

Simply running away is risky because the winner may be tempted to give chase and attack. Some animals give a clear signal to let their **opponent** know that it is beaten. For example, a chameleon signals that it has admitted defeat by losing its bright colour and turning white, like a flag of surrender. A sea anemone shows that it has lost by pulling in its tentacles and slowly sliding out of reach of its opponent.

A defeated wolf lies on its back and shows its throat and belly to its opponent. These are the most vulnerable parts of its body. By exposing them to the winner, the loser shows that it can no longer defend itself.

23

Winner takes all

The more evenly matched the **rivals** are, the more likely it is that a meeting will end in a serious fight. If neither animal is prepared to give way during the early rounds of the contest, the fighting becomes more violent. For example, if a quick bit of neck wrestling does not produce a winner, male zebras start using their hooves against each other. The fight turns into a vicious kicking contest in which a leg or jawbone can easily be broken.

Clash of the Titans

Only the fiercest bull gets to mate with all the females in a **colony** of elephant seals. When they fight, the giant bulls rear up and roar loudly. They tear at each other's flesh with their long canine teeth. One hundred females is a prize well worth fighting for. When the prize is big enough, males are prepared to risk serious injury.

> By the end of a fight between bull elephant seals, the beach is often stained red with blood.

Gangs of langur monkeys fight running battles high above the streets of Indian cities. Young males try to take over the leadership of the monkey **troop**. They attack each other with razor-sharp teeth. Eventually, the old leader will lose one of these fierce street fights. When he does, the young male who takes over the troop shows no mercy. The old leader may even die from his injuries.

In a fierce fight between two male lions, the loser has very little chance of surviving the contest.

Fights to the death

It is not unusual for an animal to die in battle or shortly after. Male lions fight for the right to take over a **pride**. It often turns into a fight to the death. Even if the defeated lion is not killed during the fight, he often dies from his wounds.

A meeting between **rival** slugs may also lead to a fight to the death. Although they look pretty harmless, slugs have a lower jaw lined with tiny, razor-sharp teeth. When they fight, they slash at each other with these teeth in order to wound their **opponent**.

Hornets and other insects often attack beehives. The worker bees will sacrifice their own lives to protect the queen and her **grubs**. Worker bees have a sting at the end of their **abdomen**, which they use to attack the hornets. But the tip of this sting is **barbed**, like a fishhook. Once they have used their sting, they cannot pull it out again without leaving behind part of their own body.

When a hungry mongoose tackles a deadly cobra, the fighting is guaranteed to last until one of them is dead.

Programmed to fight

A male Siamese fighting fish is among the world's most aggressive fish. When two males meet, they attack immediately. They will bite huge chunks out of each other and usually fight to the death. Siamese fighting fish are the perfect example of a fighting machine. Like a computer that is programmed to behave in a certain way, they cannot help themselves. They were born to be ferocious fighters.

*In **captivity**, male Siamese fighting fish have to be kept apart to stop them attacking each other.*

Fact file

The black palm cockatoo is the only bird that uses a tool to make a noise.

A fighting hippopotamus uses its teeth to gain a good hold on its **opponent** during pushing contests. Its specially designed lower jaw acts like a shock absorber.

The bigger and brighter the patch of blue skin on a mandrill's face, the older and fitter he is. This allows **rivals** to weigh up their chances of beating him before they commit themselves to a fight.

An African rhinoceros is strong enough to toss an adult horse into the air. However, it usually fights rivals by shoulder-barging and using its horn as a club. The Asian rhinoceros fights by slashing with its bottom teeth.

One blow from the swinging neck of an adult giraffe can kill a lion.

The curved horns of a giant sable antelope can grow over 1.5 metres long.

In a **colony** of elephant seals, the strongest bull can weigh up to 2.5 tonnes.

Hamadryas butterflies from South America are also known as cracker butterflies. The male hamadryas challenges other butterflies by flying into the air and making loud clicking noises with his wings.

A wildlife cameraman once filmed a fight between a deadly fer-de-lance snake and a tarantula. The contest lasted over an hour, and ended with the spider eating the snake.

When stags fight, they use their sharp, bony antlers as weapons. If an antler breaks, it will not grow back until the following year.

The ibex is a wild goat that lives in the mountains of Europe. Fighting ibex rear up on their hind legs and attack rivals with a flying headbutt.

One bite from the crunching jaws of a hyena could cripple or even kill an enemy, such as a lion or leopard.

Glossary

abdomen the back end of an insect

barbed with a point like an arrow or fish-hook

breeding season time of year when animals mate

captivity when an animal is taken out of the wild

colony place where large numbers of the same animal gather to raise their young

dominant strongest

extended family family group that includes aunts, uncles and cousins

grub insect larva

inflict to impose anything unwelcome

jousting fighting with long, pointed weapons

leaf litter layer of dead, rotting leaves that covers a forest floor

mammal animal that feeds its young on milk from the mother's breast

mate breeding partner

mobbing ganging up and attacking

necking using the neck to fight

opponent enemy in a fight

pecking order kind of queue where the strongest go first and the weakest last

predator animal that hunts and kills other living creatures

pride family of lions

ritual combat fighting to test strength without risking serious injury

rival competitor in a contest, usually between males

savannah flat open area of grassland and low plants, with hardly any trees

scavenge to feed on scraps or garbage

tactic a plan for achieving something

territory area that an animal views as its own private land

threat display warning to other animals not to come too close

trespasser someone who enters an area that belongs to someone else

troop collective name for a large group of animals, especially monkeys

venom gland part of the body where a venomous animal stores its poison

Index

Titles in the *Amazing Nature* series include:

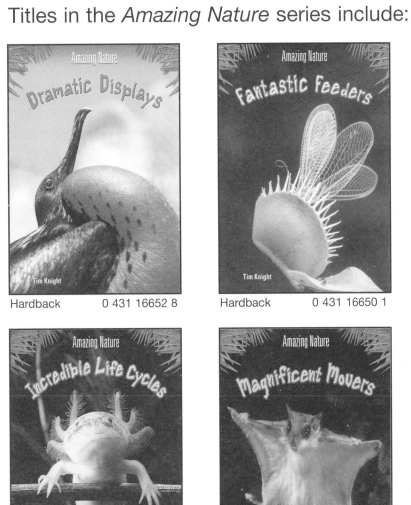

Hardback 0 431 16652 8	Hardback 0 431 16650 1	Hardback 0 431 16651 X

Hardback 0 431 16662 5	Hardback 0 431 16660 9	Hardback 0 431 16653 6

Hardback 0 431 16661 7	Hardback 0 431 16663 3

Find out about the other titles in this series on our website www.heinemann.co.uk/library